MW00581806

SRA OPEN COURT READING

The Egg

A Division of The McGraw·Hill Companies

Columbus, Ohio

www.sra4kids.com

SRA/McGraw-Hill

A Division of The **McGraw·Hill** *Companies*

Send all inquiries to:
SRA/McGraw-Hill
8787 Orion Place
Columbus, OH 43240-4027

ISBN 0-07-569408-5
1 2 3 4 5 6 7 8 9 DBH 05 04 03 02 01

On an  is a  .

island   forest

3

In the  is a .

forest   tree

4

On the  is a .

tree   branch

On the is a .

branch   nest

In the  is an egg.

nest   egg

In the 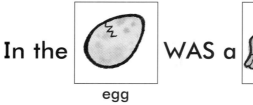 WAS a .

egg   bird